Fashions of a Decade
The 1970s

Fashions of a Decade
The
1970s

Jacqueline Herald

CHELSEA HOUSE
PUBLISHERS
An imprint of Infobase Publishing

Chelsea House
An imprint of Infobase Publishing
132 West 31st Street
New York NY 10001

Library of Congress Cataloging-in-Publication Data
Herald, Jacqueline.
Fashions of a decade. The 1970s/Jacqueline Herald
     p. cm.
     Includes bibliographical references and index
     ISBN 0-8160-6723-6 (alk. paper)
1. Clothing and dress—History—20th century—Juvenile
literature. 2. Civilization, Modern-20th century-Juvenile
literature. I. Title.
GT596.H48   2006
391.009/04-dc22   2006046807

Chelsea House books are available at special discounts when purchased in bulk quantities for businesses, associations, institutions, or sales promotions. Please call our Special Sales Department in New York at (212) 967-8800 or (800) 322-8755.

You can find Chelsea House on the World Wide Web at
http://www.chelseahouse.com

Author: Jacqueline Herald
Research for new edition: Kathy Elgin
Editor: Karen Taschek
Text design by Simon Borrough
Cover design by Dorothy M.Preston
Illustrations by Robert Price
Picture Research by Shelley Noronha

This new edition produced for Chelsea House by Bailey Publishing Associates Ltd.

Printed in China through Morris Press, Ltd.

MPL SB 10 9 8 7 6 5 4 3 2 1

This book is printed on acid-free paper.

Contents

The 70s

It was writer Tom Wolfe who dubbed the seventies the "Me Decade." The problem was, lots of "Me's" were fighting for a piece of the action. Politically extremist and fundamentalist groups committed acts of terrorism. In terms of dress, fashion magazines declared, "Anything goes." No rules applied any more.

Nostalgia and an interest in traditional cultures of the developing world were elements that ran through the decade, from radical chic to punk. Retro styles were promoted by films like *The Great Gatsby* (1974), in which Mia Farrow and Robert Redford wore twenties-style clothes, and the American TV show *Happy Days*, based on the popular film *American Graffiti*, which centered on fifties teenagers.

▼ *Grease*, one of several fifties nostalgia movies. John Travolta's greased forelock of hair is authentic enough, although the large shirt collar and cut of his draped jacket and stovepipe pants are unmistakably seventies.

Watergate and the Fall of President Nixon

On June 17, 1972, five men were arrested after attempting to remove bugging devices from the headquarters of the Democratic National Committee in the Watergate building in Washington, DC. The incident was later traced to the offices of US President Richard Nixon and led to a scandal that reverberated for several years. In May 1974 impeachment hearings against Nixon were opened; millions of Americans tuned in to the live broadcasts of the Senate Watergate hearings, which surpassed the soap operas and baseball games in popularity. In August Nixon resigned—the first US president to do so before the end of his elected term—and vice-president Gerald Ford took over at the White House. Although Nixon was granted a complete pardon for any federal crimes, many of his top aides were sent to prison.

▶On June 28, 1970, the anniversary of riots that followed a police raid on a gay bar in New York City, the Gay Liberation Front organized a march from Greenwich Village to Central Park. Since then, gay pride marches have become annual events in cities around the world and have taken on a festive, Mardi Gras-like character, often involving floats, dancers, drag queens, and loud music.

The "Me Decade"

Hard as fashion tried to promote them, elements of past styles were no escape from the very real social, political, and environmental upheavals of the present. The energy crisis; increasing unemployment and world recession; the civil rights, gay liberation, and women's movements; growing concern over the future of the environment, focusing on ecology and antinuclear strategies; demands for political recognition and independence; terrorism, bombing, and hijacking; the arrival of the computer microchip—all these elements were reflected in the way people dressed.

The world seemed smaller. The Concorde, the first supersonic airplane, took to the skies. Charter lines sprang up, offering cheap transatlantic travel, and American fast-food chains like McDonald's and Colonel Sanders's Kentucky Fried Chicken spread across Europe.

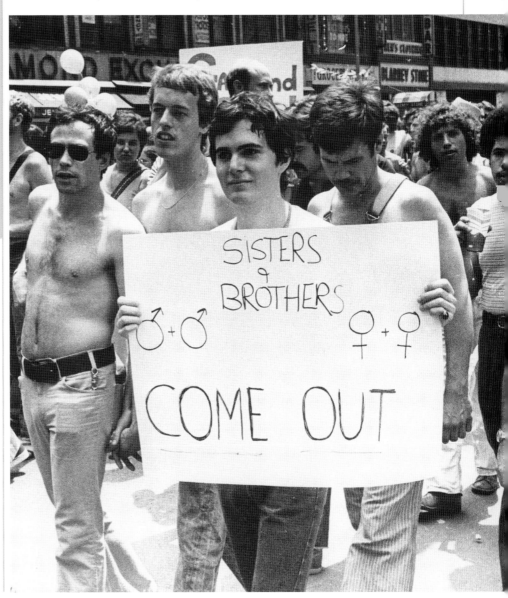

You Are What You Wear

The idea of dress as a system of signs, indicating the lifestyle and aspirations of the wearer, was taken very seriously in the 1970s. The discipline is known as semiotics. Writings by French semiologist Roland Barthes became required reading in many art colleges that prioritized theory over practice. In a 1976 essay entitled "Lumbar Thought," Italian academic and novelist Umberto Eco wrote wittily about the relationship between the internal experience and external appearance of wearing blue jeans.

American psychologists discussed the social and political implications of power dressing. Topical magazines discussed the language of status symbols, designers, and clothes. Peter York's caustic columns in the British magazine *Harpers & Queen* defined immediately identifiable social "types" like the Sloane Rangers, London's nearest equivalent to American preppies.

▼The Sloane Ranger, in her neat, almost traditional clothes, could be seen anywhere around the Chelsea district of London.

▶In March 1978, the supertanker *Amoco Cadiz* ran aground and split in two off the coast of Brittany, spilling 220,000 tons of crude oil into the English Channel. It was the worst oil spill in marine history, threatening wildlife along seventy miles of coastline.

Environmental Concerns

In 1970, BBC TV's *Doomwatch* series attracted a huge audience, covering environmental problems like the smog over New York City and Tokyo. This opened up an international debate on pollution, with concern voiced over lead poisoning from exhaust fumes and the threat to the ozone layer. In 1976, in Seveso, Italy, a cloud of dioxin was accidentally leaked from a fertilizer factory, a disaster which left people wondering about its long-term effects on local inhabitants' health.

In 1970, Americans celebrated the first Earth Day and many joined increasingly active environmental groups. However, they were working against ever-increasing problems. Acid rain began to kill trees and pollute lakes in the United States and Canada. Many urban areas, especially Los Angeles, suffered from extremely poor air quality, and water pollution closed beaches on the Great Lakes.

The Vietnam War

The decade opened with a surge of demonstrations against the Vietnam War, in which America had been actively involved since 1964. In May 1970, US forces invaded neutral Cambodia. That month, tension ran high at Ohio's Kent State University when National Guard troops fired on protesting students, four of whom were shot dead. Following America's devastating bombing campaign against the Vietcong (Communist) forces and North Vietnamese civilians in 1972, a cease-fire between the United States and North Vietnam was signed in early 1973. American civilians and troops were withdrawn, and prisoners of war returned home to a tumultuous welcome. In January of 1973 the highly controversial military draft ended in the United States. But the war was not over. In April 1975 a North Vietnamese attack on the South led speedily to the fall of Saigon and while US helicopters airlifted out US civilians and as many Vietnamese as they could carry, Communist forces completed their takeover of the country. The film *M*A*S*H*—a black comedy set in Korea but obviously referring to Vietnam—satirized war and the society that instigated it. In 1977 US President Jimmy Carter pardoned most of an estimated 10,000 draft evaders, many of whom had fled to Canada.

▲This sleek and elegant couple are wearing fashions by Christian Dior. They represent the conservative face of respectability at a time of threatening change.

▶Ron Kovic, one of the most outspoken anti-war activists, addresses the crowd at a Vietnam vets demonstration in 1972. Kovic's story was the basis of the film *Born on the Fourth of July*.

The Women's Movement

By the late sixties, "minority" groups—blacks or gay people and women—were becoming more visible and audible in the political arena. The publication of feminist texts gathered momentum during the seventies. They often discussed the position of women in society, focusing on the roles of mother, wife, and lover. Germaine Greer's *The Female Eunuch*, published in 1971, challenged traditional perceptions of femininity.

Magazines of the period did not just treat women as fashion consumers but took into account new values and lifestyles, including careers. The Japanese publication *An An*, launched in March 1970, covered Western fashion and included features on food, travel, and American ideals of women's independence. The British and US editions of *Cosmopolitan* offered frank advice on sex, how to take the initiative in meeting men, as well as information on makeup, and the body.

Radical feminists, however, were reluctant to discuss fashion and were readily stereotyped. "Conference and demonstration dress" included T-shirts with slogans, baggy jeans, practical carryall bags, and buttons in place of jewelry. Hair was worn long or short, but either way, it required (and got) minimal maintenance. Shoes were flat and square toed. Radical women did not shave their underarms or legs or wear bras. You didn't need to follow high fashion to make an impression.

Even so, fashion and fashion photography went on. But feminist magazines like the British *Spare Rib* began to question who the photographs were for. Men dominated the advertising and photography professions, yet images of women in fashionable dress or promoting a product were mainly looked at by other women. Shopping was mostly done by women, whether for themselves, their spouses, or their children.

▲ Australian feminist Germaine Greer burst onto the literary scene in 1971. Although members of the older generation were frequently outraged by her deliberately provocative statements, they could not dismiss her as an unattractive activist.

◄ Both Laura Ashley's Victorian-style country look and Ralph Lauren's Prairie collection had ruffles around the hem and were often worn with a kerchief around the head or neck and laced, mid-calf-length "granny" boots.

This high-fashion outfit from Louis Feraud's summer 1971 collection was probably not created to appeal to women themselves.

▲ *Cosmopolitan* was a breath of fresh air for many young women, tackling all the difficult subjects they felt they couldn't raise with their mothers.

An idea taken from the gay liberation movement was that stereotyped differences between male and female could be broken down by cross-dressing. This was taken up by women who wanted to make an impression in a man's world. Discarding skirts and high heels in favor of heavy boots and jeans was one way of downplaying the traditional images of femininity, which were thought to be male-imposed standards.

Women's executive dress borrowed elements from the suits of their male colleagues, like men's suit fabrics in subdued colors. For the first time in history, women's pantsuits were accepted as stylish city wear. By 1978, padded shoulders and tailored coats were popular, both reflecting the radical feminism of the early seventies and anticipating the power dressing of the yuppie eighties.

◀ Janet Reger satin underwear represented the top end of the market. However, this is the sort of suggestive photography that feminists seriously questioned.

▲ Although the use of cork in platform soles made them lighter to wear and the ankle strap held the shoe in place, shoes like this were not the best of gear for biking or scooter riding.

The Teenage Gaze

Youth subcultures—their racial identities, styles of dress and behavior, and patterns of consumption, especially in the area of music—were studied by the new wave of sociologists. Interviews and surveys revealed that teenagers, searching for a constant against which to measure themselves, paid an incredible amount of attention to detail when observing the clothing of their peers. American novelist Alison Lurie, with her own acute eye for detail, noted in 1976 that according to junior high school lore, "freaks always wear Lees, greasers wear Wranglers, and everyone else wears Levi's."

Skinheads, one type of subculture, grew out of a British group of the late sixties known as mods, a working-class reaction against middle-class hippies. Skinheads were first called all kinds of names: peanuts, skulls, boiled eggs, cropheads. The mods' hair had been cropped to less than half an inch, but the skinhead crop was the most severe haircut you could get. Skinheads looked neat yet aggressive. They stomped around in tight, short pants (permanent press or bleached Levi's), crombies (three-quarter-length wool coats), suspenders, plain or striped Ben Sherman shirts with button-down collars, and big, highly polished

Terrorism Strikes

Political protest turned violent, resulting in the hijacking of airplanes and bombing campaigns. The seventies opened with Black September—four successive hijackings by breakaway Palestinian groups—and 1972 saw Bloody Sunday in Northern Ireland; the massacre of innocent Israelis by Palestinian guerrillas at the Munich Olympic Games; and a car-bombing campaign by the young revolutionary Baader-Meinhof organization in West Germany. Many of these struggles went on throughout the decade: 1979 ended with 90 people held hostage at the American embassy in Iran by military followers of the Ayatollah Khomeini.

work boots (Doc Martens) that, for a true skinhead, had to have eight eyelets. Skinhead girls wore a "feather" haircut, cropped on top with wispy tufts framing the face and neck. "Suedeheads" were identifiable by their grown-out crops, sometimes sideburns, and short coats or workmen's jackets.

Economy Drives

In the early 1970s, the numbers of unemployed and of full-time students rose in the West. By 1975, the world was in recession: unemployment figures had been

▲Terrorism hit the Paris runways in winter 1978–79 with Daniel Hechter's IRA tweed look—black beret, leather jacket, man's shirt with button-down collar, and narrow black tie. The roll-down ankle socks worn over stockings were a young woman's fashion inspired by roller-skating gear. Here they are worn with heavy, crepe-soled, tongued brogues.

▶It was often hard to tell the difference between boys and girls in the skinhead world: many of the clothes were interchangeable.

rising steadily, along with inflation, for a number of years, and demand for manufactured goods had decreased. The energy crisis of 1973–74 put extra pressure on the manufacturing industry to reduce overhead. By the end of the decade, the number of people employed in fashion-related industries dropped in the West, matched by a dramatic fall in trade union membership. However, the number of homeworkers was increasing, especially among the immigrant population. At the same time, recession meant that industry was reluctant to invest in fast-changing technology—it was far cheaper to use labor from the developing world.

Consequently, the global balance shifted as multinational corporations financed from the West manufactured more products in the Far East, taking full advantage of the free trade zones. These areas were centered on ports into which raw materials or component parts could be imported, then assembled and re-exported without paying duties and without complying with trade union agreements or industrial legislation. Many women and children were exploited, especially in the clothing and textile industries.

The long-term political and cultural implications were considerable. For the past century, the industrialized West had been treated as the model for developing countries. Now, in its place, Japan entered the vanguard of microtechnology and industrial organization—and prospered.

▲The drum majorette look. Charlie's Angel Farrah Fawcett is the picture of American health with her long blonde hair, broad smile, and perfect teeth.

More Dash Than Cash

As job prospects dwindled, a network of street markets developed for the sale of secondhand clothes. New clothes were made from old. Old and new were worn together, often in unexpected combinations of color, pattern, and texture or of men's and women's clothing. *Cheap Chic*, a guide to "hundreds of money-saving

▲The glamorous Shirley Bassey, worldwide cabaret star and voice of the James Bond theme songs, clearly had no concerns about the anti-fur lobby. Here she is wearing a fur hat and coat and crocodile skin pants.

hints to create your own great look," was a big seller. Its authors declared, "Fashion as a dictatorship of the elite is dead."

New aesthetics emerged. Some were achieved with the help of products from the kitchen or bathroom cabinet. People dyed their own T-shirts, sometimes batiking or tie-dyeing them for a late hippie look. Punk girls dyed their grandfathers' long johns black, starting a fashion for leggings that would develop into the high-fashion Lycra versions of the 1980s. Boys customized their hair gels to hold the spikes in place. For the perfect "hedgehog," Tony James of the band Generation X used a combination of lemon juice, spit, and orange juice, admitting, "I used to walk round smelling like a carton of Kia-Ora [orange drink]."

Small Is Beautiful

In unison with the earth's atmosphere, the debates about ecology and appropriate and alternative technologies were heating up. Ecology became a political bandwagon: parties like the German Greens and environmental lobby groups like Friends of the Earth and Greenpeace were established. *The Greening of America* (1970), by Yale University law professor Charles Reich, predicted that US society would change permanently for the better because American youth would attach greater importance to conserving the beauty of their environment than to social status and financial success. In 1973, the book *Small Is Beautiful* by prophet of intermediate technology E. F. Schumacher was published and supported by lecture tours and a promotional campaign.

Concern was also growing about the world's endangered animals. Georgina Howell wrote in a 1975 issue of British *Vogue*: "No woman with her eyes open would walk about now in the skins of a rare animal and be the butt of raised eyebrows and uncomplimentary remarks."

Take Care of Yourself

Momentous breakthroughs were taking place in science and medicine. The seventies boasted the first test-tube baby and advances in ultrasound and in organ transplants. At the same time, interest in alternative medicine was growing; a group of American doctors visited China in 1971 to study acupuncture. Diet and exercise gained an even more prominent place in health care.

Energy Crisis

The Arab oil embargo that followed the Yom Kippur war of 1973 led to an increase in the price of oil. In the United States long lines formed at gas stations—if there was any gas at all, for many stations ran out. In Britain the world energy crisis was compounded by a shortage of coal stocks, due to an overtime ban by miners; as a result, industry was restricted to three days' per week electricity supply. Suddenly the power to drive machinery and heat water, as well as to fuel cars and planes, seemed more precious. Oil-based products like synthetic yarns and certain types of plastics increased in price. For economic reasons—the environmental advantages were only coincidental—the manufacturing and auto industries started to investigate energy-saving technologies. Research into solar, wind, and geothermal power was stepped up, though unfortunately much of this initiative was abandoned as soon as the oil embargo ended.

◄ Jogging became an obsession. For some it was an excuse to bare all, while others, like the woman behind, preferred to cover up in sweat-pants.

Black Roots

In 1970, the African American tennis player Arthur Ashe was refused a visa to play in the South African championships. The politics of race not only entered the sports arena, but TV and cinema, too. *Roots*, the TV version of Alex Haley's book in which the author traced his ancestry to West Africa in the early days of the slave trade, was a US sensation in 1977. The program boosted African Americans' sense of cultural identity and inspired many to visit or settle in Africa. Movies made specifically for black audiences, such as Melvin Van Peebles' *Sweet Sweetback's Baadasssss Song* and the *Shaft* films, offered important images for African American 1970s culture.

▲Thea Porter's interpretation of exotic Eastern dress, with short bolero jacket and full skirt with paisley motif. These silk-and-silver clothes were in a class above the casual hippie's Indian block prints and embroidered gauze.

As a result of the cholesterol debate, new low-fat spreads appeared in the supermarket. Magazines and bookstores were flooded with literature on dieting and food. More people were becoming vegetarians. The fashionable districts of many cities now included health food stores and restaurants and an occasional juice bar.

Sales of sportswear and exercise bikes boomed. As many more amateurs began running marathons, James F. Fixx's *The Complete Book of Running* became a best seller. Health and "natural" good looks were turning into big business. Health clubs were on the increase, offering swimming pools, saunas, yoga and exercise classes, massage, and steam rooms.

Slimming down, by whatever agonizing means, was widespread in the seventies. A woman with the ideal slender figure had no problem burning her bra. At the beginning of the decade, natural was a key word in cosmetics advertising. Estée Lauder launched a line called "Little Nothings." To turn blue eyes green or brown eyes bluer, the latest optical fashion of 1972 was a pair of tinted contact lenses.

Craft Revival

The seventies saw a revitalized interest in crafts like jewelry, ceramics, knitting, embroidery, and screen printing on textiles. National and federal councils were set up to promote the crafts, especially the one-of-a-kind items designed and made by art school graduates. New magazines and craft galleries promoted the fine-art approach to the fiber arts. They offered an alternative to mass-produced goods, yet at the same time, many craftspeople hoped that their designs would be put into mass production, thus closing the gap between design and industry.

▲Ed Asner and Levar Burton starred in *Roots*, one of the seminal TV programs of the seventies.

▲In the London men's boutique Hung On You, colorful silk caftans are offset by the strikingly patterned rugs imported from Central Asia.

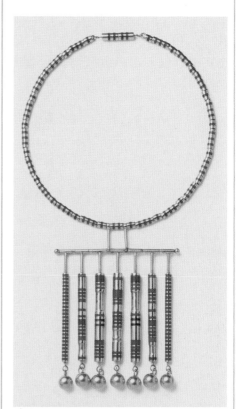

▲The ethnic collections of museums like London's Victoria and Albert were searched for items like this rare gold necklace, which was used as a model for "new" designs.

The fashion for handmade clothes and individualistic decoration also embraced the imported traditional and tourist crafts of developing nations of the world, contributing to the ethnic look of the early seventies.

The Art Market

Partly due to the alliance between Pop Art and advertising, thanks to Andy Warhol's Factory, the art market became increasingly associated with the promotion of products. Some of the most avant-garde ideas were to be found in advertising photography and were concerned less about what the product looked like than about the attitude with which it was worn or used.

▶ Stripes were everywhere in the mid-seventies, usually going in different directions. Here oversized scarves and knitted hats with a home-knit look are worn with striped socks and strapped wedge sandals.

Some new art forms entered the galleries from the street. Graffiti was sprayed or splattered on the sides of subway cars or on walls in the poorer sections of large cities. In New York City, Fab Five Freddy—named after the number 5 subway trains on which he lived and "worked"—became the medium's star performer. Freddy was also a prophet of 1980s hip-hop, rap, and break dancing.

On the West Coast, rock posters were celebrated in a show held at the San Francisco Museum of Modern Art in 1976. Artists like David Hockney, Allen Jones, Patrick Hughes, and Elizabeth Frink became involved in T-shirt design, while Italian knitwear manufacturer Missoni invited painters into the studios to give a new impetus to fashion.

"Art School," a song about individualism and rebelliousness, was performed by the band The Jam in 1977. None of The Jam had actually been to art school, but many rock musicians had. David Byrne, lead singer of Talking Heads, formed in 1975, had studied at the Rhode Island School of Design in Providence. No wonder that the visual arts and performance were directly linked and that some rock music of the period was influenced by movements in the fine arts.

The Music Business

New sounds and musical forms were often a reaction against the conventions of romantic, melodic lyrics. The soul music of performers like J. B. Sly certainly was. Some music made a deliberate but artificial attempt to project the voice of "the people." In this way, soccer fans' songs were built into the background chorus of British hit songs by Slade and Gary Glitter. Punk singers like Johnny Rotten of the Sex Pistols developed an explicitly working-class voice by using lower-class accents and being deliberately inarticulate. Through the seventies, British bands were drawing inspiration from West Indian ska and reggae music. And new developments in audio technology, notably synthesizers and tape recorders, also contributed to the variety.

▲Nobody does stripes like Missoni. The company, run by Ottavio and Rosita Missoni, was making a name for itself for its imaginative use of distinctively patterned knit fabrics.

◀Isaac Hayes and The Emotions—the glamorous face of soul. Sometimes, black women played down their color, straightened their hair, and tinted it with henna. On the whole, the range of cosmetics specifically for black skins was still limited.

▶Jimmy Page of Led Zeppelin, seen here in soft, clinging satin. The huge flares, cut long and wide around the hem to accommodate platform shoes, made hips and thighs look extra slim. Hand-painted flowers like these adorned ties, scarves, and vests.

The rock media were beginning to discuss music in the broader context of style. One of the most influential figures in this area was Tom Wolfe, who wrote for America's *Rolling Stone* magazine, and following his example, British journalists began arguing for more space in the established weeklies, *Melody Maker* and *New Musical Express*. New magazines appeared, some promoting the popular side of the music business while others, known as "fanzines," covered the underground scene.

By the mid-1970s worldwide music sales grossed well over $4 billion annually—more than the film industry or sports. In *Solid Gold*, a study of the American rock industry, R. Serge Denisoff divided the audience into three groups: young, predominantly female, bubble-gum pop fans (who bought singles and posters to hang on their bedroom walls); older "punk rockers" (rock as aggressive background music for rituals of dancing, dating, and getting stoned on weekends); and collegians ("folk-art-rock" concertgoers and LP listeners, who enjoyed good lyrics).

▲ABBA was one of the most astounding success stories of the seventies music scene, achieving worldwide fame overnight as a result of winning the Eurovision Song Contest in 1974 with "Waterloo." Although their stage outfits fell into the glam-rock category, their general image was wholesome and had universal appeal.

Teenyboppers enjoyed the Osmonds, David Cassidy, and the tartan-clad Bay City Rollers; sales of their records boomed. The Jackson Five, in which Michael Jackson got his start, was the seventies' biggest-selling group on the Motown label.

Success depended on image as well as performance. The phenomenal international success of the Swedish group ABBA was as much due to the singers' image as to the new quality of their sound.

New Technology

In 1970 the first microprocessor was patented by Intel, and the first cheap pocket calculators were retailed in the United States. Experiments with tele-shopping began, and people pondered the dramatic changes of lifestyle that these advances might bring. Would supermarkets and fashion boutiques soon become institutions of the past? Auto-focus cameras and microchip-programmed washing machines were the new "necessities." Matt black digital watches were novel—expensive at first, but thanks to British inventor Clive Sinclair they came down in price, and by the end of the decade Japanese versions were flooding the mass market. In 1979 Sony launched the Walkman. The microprocessor brought information to one's fingertips, but it was the leather-bound Filofax personal filing system that brought it into style.

▶The Jackson Five in the mid-seventies, with lead singer Michael, seen here center front. They have afro hairstyles, and their medley of shirts are homemade from women's dress prints, lampshade fringing, and striped furnishing fabric.

Fashion Rules Okay?

Although it was generally agreed that design added spice to life, real haute couture was increasingly being dismissed as anachronistic—"a degenerate institution propped up by a sycophantic press," declared fashion writer Kennedy Fraser in 1975. To survive, established fashion houses like Christian Dior and Yves Saint Laurent were designing more and more ready-to-wear collections and catering to the more casual and practical moods of the moment.

Vogue announced: "There are no rules in the fashion game now." In the early 1970s, the magazine featured a vegetable gardener wearing a beret, a scarf, wrinkled woolly tights, and a loose knitted mohair coat and commented, "The clothes aren't smart, but they're much in fashion."

Nostalgia played a major role throughout the decade. Walking into the Biba store in London was like stepping back in time. In the dim Art Deco- and Art Nouveau-style lighting, between Edwardian lampshades dripping with fringes and huge potted plants reflected in the metallic sheen of the Deco wallpaper and mirrors, you could sink into a plum-colored sofa and wait for a friend. Meanwhile, you watched passersby try on feather boas and bias-cut scarves, pulling down cloche hats well below the eyebrows until nothing showed but a dark, plum-colored mouth.

The boutique culture of the sixties continued reasonably successfully, although influential shops like Biba did not last the decade. However, department stores were beginning to fill up with little individual shops, each devoted to an

▲ A classic example of exotic style in fashion and furnishings. This model can barely be distinguished from the sea of leopard skins from which she is emerging.

▶Menswear by Pierre Cardin, 1973–74. Functional elements of sports clothing, like zippers and knee patches, were exaggerated to make bold fashion statements. The black-and-white houndstooth check might previously have been made into a jacket or trousers but was never before worn like this.

▼Denzel Washington as Steve Biko and Kevin Kline as journalist Donald Woods in the 1987 film *Cry Freedom*.

Human Rights

As the struggle for human rights pervaded the world, the message of the politically oppressed was expressed in a variety of ways. In 1970 Alexander Solzhenitsyn's novels addressing the struggles of humans in a representative political system won him the Nobel Prize for literature. The next year, two films re-evaluating the relations between American Indians and whites were released: *Little Big Man* and *Soldier Blue*. In 1977 Steve Biko, a black trade union leader and a founder of the Black Consciousness Movement, was found dead in a South African police cell. His death provoked major international concern and criticism of the South African regime.

individual designer. Henri Bendel of New York was one of the first stores to do this in 1970, opening outlets for Thea Porter and Sonia Rykiel clothes.

The revolution in men's fashion retailing took the big stores by storm. Men's boutiques in these big stores sold the latest lines and fabrics. Those that sold internationally found that preferences in menswear varied from one branch to another. Navy velvet men's suits sold very well in Paris, perhaps, but not in London; Frenchmen preferred one center-back vent in the jacket, while the British liked two. Just as haute couture for women was almost a thing of the past, so traditional custom-made tailoring was under threat. Some tailors launched ready-to-wear collections abroad, particularly in Japan.

Tightening the purse strings was necessary for most people in response to the energy crisis and recession. Dedicated followers of fashion with less money

◄ A pink evening dress by Clovis Ruffin displays all the simple elegance for which he was noted.

▲Lilies add a fin de siècle elegance to this Art Nouveau-style flowered pantsuit for evening wear.

to spend were buying more imported clothing, while others opted out and stepped into jeans. The rare breed who had cash chose to flaunt it in the luxury of Parisian couture, proving that they were immune to financial crises. This left homegrown designers and manufacturers in a vacuum.

Up-and-coming designers began to pave new ways forward. Clovis Ruffin (Ruffinwear) clothes appealed "to the sort of people who are not frightened of pulling things over their hairdos." He used the new generation of silky synthetic jersey fabrics in subtle plain colors to produce simply constructed, zipperless dresses that could be dressed down or up with plastic or diamonds. Also exploring the aesthetics of new manufacturing technology, Stephen Burrows was the first designer of note to use zigzag machine stitching in an obvious way, as structure and decoration.

▲Vivienne Westwood and Malcolm McLaren, arch-priests of punk. Westwood is wearing one of her own leather creations.

Jubilee Year

On June 7, 1977, Silver Jubilee street parties all over Britain celebrated twenty-five years of Queen Elizabeth's reign. It was no coincidence that, in the same year, the shop Sex—owned by purveyors of punk Vivienne Westwood and Malcolm McLaren—was renamed Seditionaries, indicating Westwood's belief that people must be seduced into revolt. As an anti-Establishment gesture, they produced the "God Save the Queen" T-shirt, featuring Jamie Reid graphics in which a portrait of the Queen was defaced. It was promptly banned. Derek Jarman's film *Jubilee*, released in the same year, was another chance to shock, mixing images of conservatism, like a pastel-colored twin sweater set such as the queen might wear, with black leather and rubber.

28

Tough Guys

Get Stoned

A sixties leftover, long hair for men still represented a counterculture image. While the Establishment might no longer have been shocked by the disheveled hippie style, with its suggestion of poverty and irresponsibility, it didn't quite trust longhairs either. "Treat this man with respect, he may have just sold a million records," read the framed poster of a downbeat hippie, hanging in the lobby of the Continental Hyatt House hotel on Sunset Boulevard, Los Angeles.

In the United States, the Grateful Dead were the best living monuments to hippie style. Rich European hippies flew to Amsterdam to buy drugs and long leather coats, while London's Kensington Market outfitted them with imported Afghan coats, Indian embroidered or printed blouses and gauzy skirts, and unisex velvet loons (pants that flared below the knee).

It was a body-conscious society. The Rolling Stones' zipper-flyed *Sticky Fingers* album cover of 1971, designed by Andy Warhol, teased the group's fans about that. And if sex, drink, and drugs were on everybody's mind, they were the making and breaking of Jim Morrison, lead singer of The Doors, who died of an alcohol and drug overdose in 1971.

Morrison's fashion of leather pants, however, lived on for some time and, as ever, leather jackets signified tough guys. They were worn by heavy metal headbangers, whose heroes were hard rock groups like Motörhead, Status Quo, and Lynyrd Skynyrd. Denim, daubed with painted images and names of rock icons or encrusted with studs, was an alternative to leather.

▲Variations on the denim theme: patchwork denim shoulder bag, wraparound skirt worn with tight crinkle-cotton shirt, and jeans (now cut for women) tucked into knee-length boots.

◄ The Grateful Dead, seen here in relatively restrained style. Throughout their long career, the group toured constantly, promoting a true hippie sense of community among their fans, who were known as "Deadheads." In 1973 they played to an estimated 600,000 people at the Summer Jam at Watkins Glen.

►Weekend hippies taking a country walk. His afghan coat with embroidery trim is one of the defining garments of the seventies. Cheap versions, imported from various parts of Asia, were famous for smelling strongly when they got damp because the sheepskin had not been cured properly.

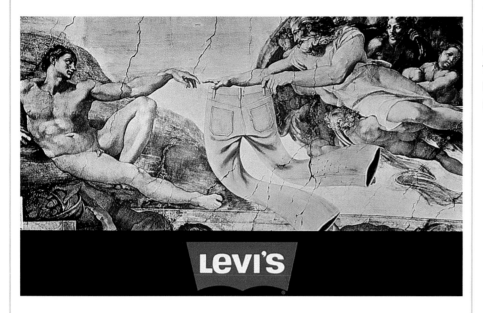

Radical Denim

While denim was a kind of uniform, it could also be manipulated or embellished to make a highly individual statement. Levi's jackets were customized with embroidered stars and stripes and super-studded names and messages. One jacket even had an ashtray built into the sleeve!

Traditional blue denim, dyed in indigo, was guaranteed to fade. Fading signified wear and tear and, by implication, hard work. New clothes made from old denim passed as fashion and sold in boutiques at high prices. They included skirts and flared pants made from jeans by opening up part of the original seam and inserting a triangular gusset.

Besides blue, new colors and finishes were introduced, mostly inspired by the worn-out look. Brushed denim simulated the "velvet" feel of an old pair of jeans, and colors tended to look drab and washed out: beige-pink, pale blue, and nondescript tan. Stonewashing—which means exactly what it says, putting new jeans into a pebble-filled washing machine—broke down the even color and starchiness of new cloth. Alternatively, a new pair of jeans could be worn in a bath of salty water until they felt skintight. Some dress-weight novelty denims were woven with jaunty patterns of teddy bears, flowers, and checks.

Denim was even copied in other cloths. In 1972, designer Henry Lehr produced leather suits dyed in denim blue that were much more expensive than the real thing. Gradually, a reaction against denim set in, with corduroy becoming a popular alternative for pants and blouson-style jackets.

And so, within the language of denim, were clear distinctions, both in terms of how much was spent on any one outfit and in how you wore and treated your jeans. Rich women walked up New York City's stylish Madison Avenue with their well-cut jeans neatly pressed, perhaps accessorized by a silk shirt and famous French label scarf, whereas young students might hang out in New York's Greenwich Village in faded and patched jeans topped with a T-shirt or Indian block-printed cotton blouse.

▲ Bruce Springsteen's appearance on the cover of his album *Darkness on the Edge of Town* is a seventies update of the James Dean look: white T-shirt, black leather jacket, and blue jeans still symbolized the urban rebel.

Lumberjacks and Cowboys Are All Right

A number of stores began to specialize in western styles, selling cowboy boots and other items. The fashion for tucking jeans into boots became part of the seventies' "look." The often intricate tooled patterns on rawhide belts were just the kind of craft that the hippies of rural communes made and sold to supplement their vegetable-growing economy.

The tough-guy image promoted by lumberjack and cowboy clothes was consciously adopted by the gay community on the West Coast. It was popularized in the later 1970s, when The Village People, a disco squad, dressed up as macho men: cop, construction worker, biker, and cowboy. Versions of this look have persisted as the corporate image of the gay fraternity: the handlebar mustache, plaid lumberjack shirt, tight blue jeans, field boots, and short, GI-style cropped hair.

To writer Tom Wolfe, radical chic meant wearing secondhand "jeans of the people—hod carrier jeans—at the Army surplus at two pairs for twenty-nine cents." The surplus store was also the place to go for camouflage and khaki army fatigues.

▼Members of the Village People parodying the most macho images: uniformed air force officers, bikers in black leather gear, cowboys and Indians, and construction workers.

Nostalgia

Retro Chic

Secondhand clothes did not have to look sad and drab—they could also be glamorous. The flashier side of thrift shopping was in San Francisco, where stores like Casey's Faded World dressed up the glitzy transvestite and gay scene. Their style was epitomized in the early seventies by a group called the Cockettes. On London's King's Road, you could walk out of Granny Takes a Trip looking like a Beatle from the *Sgt. Pepper* album cover. The shop sold the distinctive red uniforms of the Chelsea Pensioners—retired army personnel living just down the road at the Chelsea Hospital—and round gold-rimmed "granny glasses," like those worn by John Lennon.

Rock Back the Clock

Nostalgia was big business. One major influence on the seventies came from the fifties. Elvis, the king of rock, influenced the style and performance of musicians and singers and also captivated the public at large. In 1974, Colin Irwin wrote in *Melody Maker*: "Retailers of soft goods last year sold more than $20,000,000 worth of Presley products. Chain, drug-, and novelty stores now feature lipsticks in autographed cases bearing color names for such Presley hit tunes as Hound Dog Orange, Loving You Fuchsia, and Heartbreak Pink."

Tradition for Sale

Fashions from the 1970s were based on the 1920s, 1930s, and 1940s. Hollywood produced period films conjuring up past styles that people rushed to emulate, particularly *The Godfather* and *The Great Gatsby*. Under the direction of Diana Vreeland, a former editor of *Vogue*, the Costume Institute at New York's Metropolitan Museum of Art staged major exhibitions of costume history, beginning with a retrospective of the Spanish couturier Cristóbal Balenciaga.

Laura Ashley, Ralph Lauren, punk, and New Wave fashions all shared elements of nostalgia, but clearly the motivations behind their use of the past were very different. Differences between authentic secondhand clothes and the contemporary designs based on them were also obvious. Yves Saint Laurent and other Paris designers drew on classic lines from the 1930s and 1940s, using tweeds, crepes, gabardines, and gauzier silks for formal daytime and romantic

▲A publicity photo for London's Biba boutique. The subdued coloring resembles an old sepia print and conveys an atmosphere of nostalgia that matches Biba's blend of Art Nouveau and Art Deco.

▶Mia Farrow and Robert Redford in a scene from the double-Oscar-winning *The Great Gatsby*, one of the biggest movies of 1974. Mia Farrow's wardrobe of elegant silk and lace outfits, re-created with meticulous attention to detail by the costume department, sparked off a romantic 1920s revival.

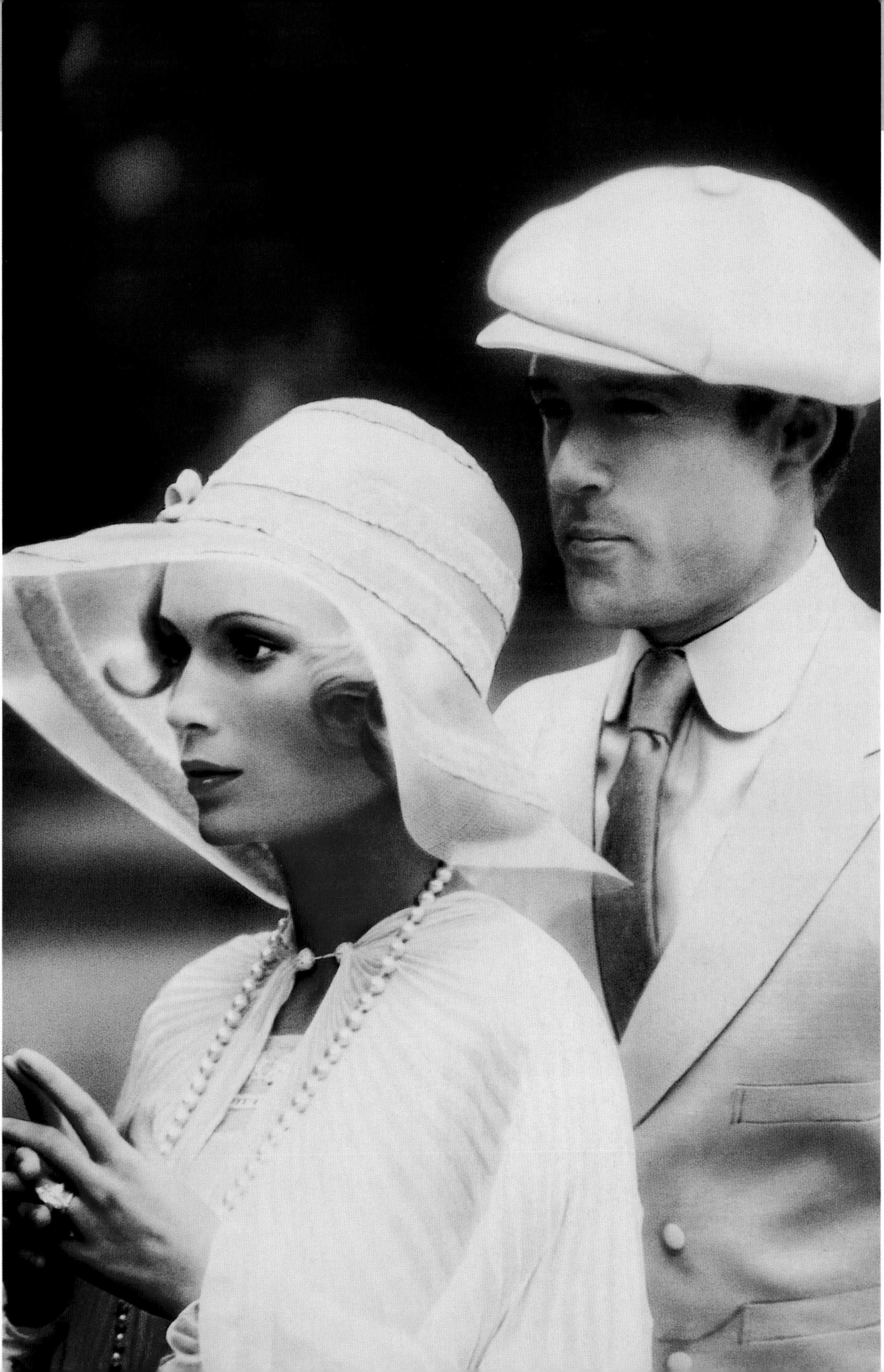

◀ Yves Saint Laurent's collections took inspiration from the East, from Romania to Mongolia. It was the traditional skills of the embroiderers he employed that distinguished the Paris haute couture industry from the ready-to-wear collections.

▼ Screen-printed fabric designs like the one on this culotte dress were often large in scale. Most outfits could be given an extra touch of style by a relatively cheap gilt metal belt in the form of disks or chain links.

evening wear. However, they still had the superb cut and finish expected of haute couture.

In contrast, Laura Ashley made inexpensive printed cotton dresses based on late Victorian and Edwardian styles, featuring ruffles around the neckline and hem, leg-of-mutton sleeves, touches of lace, tucks, buttons, and sashes. These dresses had a much less sophisticated and more rustic look, almost like dresses made at home.

The American counterpart of Laura Ashley and Liberty print dresses was Ralph Lauren's "Prairie" look of 1978. Based on the dresses described in Sears, Roebuck catalogs of the 1880s, a Prairie look dress was typically made of calico or gingham with a ruffled hem, reminiscent of early American settlers' clothing. Lauren's version was worn with layered petticoats. Meanwhile, American preppie and Ivy League styles had become popular in Japan, where the boutiques of Tokyo's Harajuku district sold reworked versions of traditional British and American looks. Wedge shoes and open-toed sandals may have echoed the wartime styles of the 1940s, but they were freshly designed, and would turn into platform soles.

Exotica

The traditional clothing of other cultures was another source of inspiration. Paris designer Hanae Mori, who opened a New York salon in the early 1970s, based many of her designs on the simple shapes and bold decoration of kimono, and costumes for traditional Japanese Noh theater. Yves Saint Laurent designed a series of Russian jackets fastened with frogging (loops). The hippies had led a trail not only to India and the East but also to North Africa, and the djellabah, a Moroccan-type hooded cloak, was the basis for some new coat shapes, while dramatic Eastern clothes and textile hangings inspired the caftan.

Eastern European folk costume inspired the fashion for gauze smocks with embroidered yokes and full sleeves gathered at the wrists. Women wore these with triangular scarves covering their hair and knotted at the back of the neck, known as *babushkas* ("grandmothers" in Russian). Men wore red-and-white printed kerchiefs, known as bandannas, or genuine Indian block-printed squares, casually knotted around the neck or around the head, like a swashbuckling Hollywood pirate.

▲This woman has created her own individual style from a combination of ethnic and "granny" elements. She's wearing a Peruvian poncho, knitted in natural cream and brown alpaca wool, as a skirt, and has paired it with a homemade shawl, crocheted from odds and ends of colored yarn, and soft leather cuffed ankle boots.

Black is Beautiful

"Afro" Roots

The afro hairstyle, symbolizing black culture and "Africanness," began as a countercultural statement and was then adopted as fashion, with figures like African American rights campaigner Angela Davis as the style leaders.

In 1973, Naomi Sims, an African American model, changed her career and began manufacturing wigs aimed specifically at black women. Each style was given an African name. Three years later, she published a book on black beauty, encouraging black women to be themselves. "You do not necessarily have to wear daishikis to prove you are proud of being black," she wrote, her message echoing the lyrics of James Brown's late 1960s hit: "Say it loud—I'm black and I'm proud." But afro wigs soon became a white fashion accessory.

Soul Princes

Although the radical chic of white Americans was partly inspired by the Black Panther look, the streetwise African American youth of the inner cities hardly aspired to looking downbeat. In a society where they were closed out of prestigious jobs and

▲Funky chic flaunted by members of Graham Central Station. Formed in San Francisco in late 1972 around an ex-member of Sly and the Family Stone, they carried on that group's attempts to promote the 1960s hippie dream of universal love in a racially integrated band.

◀ The afro hairstyle quickly became part of the white fashion agenda. Men too nervous to have their hair permed or whose hair wouldn't naturally take to the style bought wigs.

▲The cover of Funkadelic's 1970 album, *Free Your Mind and Your Ass Will Follow.*

▲James Brown, whose image was one of the most potent influences on fashionable black American youth.

restricted from buying or renting houses in better neighborhoods, cars and clothes became status symbols. For them, the style of stars like James Brown, Nancy Wilson, and Diana Ross, who had made the international charts and achieved great financial success, was the most influential. The James Brown look had nothing to do with army fatigues and everything to do with ruffled shirts, black-belted leather pieces, and bell-bottom trousers.

Social commentator Tom Wolfe described the black "soul princes" of New Haven, Connecticut, proudly strutting their stuff along Dixwell Avenue "wearing their two-tone patent Pyramids with the five-inch heels that swell out at the bottom to match the Pierre Chareau Art Deco plaid bell-bottom baggies they have on with the three-inch-deep elephant cuffs tapering upward toward the 'spray-can fit' in the seat and the black hat with the four-inch turn-down brim and the six-inch pop-up crown with the golden chain-belt hatband". From Wolfe's description it is clear that young African Americans of the seventies were as far ahead in the funky chic style game as their nineties cousins would be.

Caribbean Culture

In the seventies, West Indian culture made its presence felt in style and performance in a number of ways. On one hand, carnival was exuberant, but the other face of black style was cool, lingering in the shadows—a style cultivated in the 1960s from the American "soul brother" image of a loose-limbed figure in tight-fitting gear, moving to the offbeat of jazz, ska, and rhythm and blues.

When it came to style, the Rastafarian movement's religious roots became obscured in reggae music. Rastafarians are members of a West Indian, particularly Jamaican, group that rejects Western culture and regards Haile Selassie, the emperor of Ethiopia overthrown by a military coup in 1974, as divine. As for style, Rastas were recognized by their dreadlocks of long hair, and the colors of the Ethiopian flag: red, green and gold. These colors were deeply symbolic because the accession of Haile Selassie to the Abyssinian (Ethiopian) throne in 1930 foreshadowed the imminent downfall of white colonialism—and the liberation of black peoples. Items of dress might be decorated in the three colors: buttons, cardigans, shirts, sandals, tams (knitted or crocheted woolen hats), and walking sticks.

▲Bob Marley, one of the world's greatest reggae musicians, wearing his trademark symbols of Rastafarianism: dreadlocks and a knitted vest in the colors of the Ethiopian flag.

Northern Soul

American soul music exported to Europe and sold through specialist record shops developed several distinctive, if obscure, cult followings. They turned American soul upside down and inside out, creating something quite un-American that opened a new chapter in the history of subcultures.

One of these was a short-lived cult called "northern soul," centered on clubs in northern England like the Wigan Casino around 1972. It was a truly underground, secret activity, involving working-class kids in a life of all-night dancing. The jerky rhythms of solo dance acts, pumped up by amphetamines—pills were very much part of the cult—broke into incredible back flips, handsprings, and midair whirls. These soul dancers had close-cropped hair, clinging vests, madly flapping wide trousers, and buttons with slogans like "Keep the Faith."

▶Donna Summer, one of the most romantic and glamorous African-American singers. Her string of dance-along hits throughout the seventies earned her the title "Queen of Disco."

Glamour

Glam Rock

The term *glam rock* refers to seventies rock performances that built pure glamour into the act. Bryan Ferry and Roxy Music, David Bowie, Rod Stewart, Marc Bolan, and Elton John are the best-known "glam rockers." Beneath the sparkling surface were undercurrents of sexual innuendo, ranging from the outright campiness of the cult film *The Rocky Horror Picture Show* (1972) to the artful seduction of Roxy Music—a name derived from "Rock Sexy."

As the more successful rock stars got richer and more glamorous, so their fantasies built up into an ominous stage power. Making the dress and the act more glamorous seemed to bridge the gap between rock and pop. Style carried a high price and reaped generous rewards in the spin-offs from records.

Right at the beginning of the decade, Roxy Music's album covers married women's fashion with male rock performance. On the *For Your Pleasure* cover, model Amanda Lear offered a look-but-don't-touch image, as if she had just stepped out of some high-society portrait. The man behind Roxy Music's dress style was London designer Antony Price.

David Bowie

The most successfully packaged glam rock star was David Bowie, who hit the charts with a series of five LPs between 1971 and 1974. He was also known as Ziggy Stardust, although that was only one of a rapidly shifting sequence of personalities, looks, and stage sets. No sooner did fans copy the original Ziggy

◀ Glitter was great, whether it was on the body or on the face. Here sequins have been sewn onto skin-hugging tops of transparent net, but those not quite brave enough to bare all stuck sequined patches on the face and applied glitter eye makeup.

▶Rod Stewart stalks the stage, his "rooster" haircut and fake leopard skin jacket worn with a tight black T-shirt and casually knotted neckerchief.

▼David Bowie in his Ziggy Stardust phase. The slinky asymmetry of the body stocking and feather boa created a deliberately ambiguous, androgynous image that somehow managed to be glamorous and not camp.

haircut than Bowie was onto his next incarnation, on the *Aladdin Sane* album of 1973. By then there were plenty of Ziggy boys and girls standing at bus stops and hanging around record stores, waiting for the next Bowie album, their hair dyed green or orange, their eyelids brushed with glitter.

The definitive Ziggy haircut made the hair stand on end like a little red rooster, with a puffball in front and razored into the nape of the neck behind. The "Rooster" and the longer "Shag" version were copied by other stars, including Gary Glitter and Rod Stewart.

Bowie's disguise was a cover-up for his shyness. The look was calculatedly androgynous and artificial. What he was doing was the exact opposite of what the feminists were aiming for. They were playing down appearance, rejecting glamour, but Bowie and other stars flaunted it.

All That Glitters

While some male rock stars also toyed with the androgynous look, others followed the overt sexuality of heavy metal Led Zeppelin's lead singer Robert Plant. But even the most macho of acts in the early seventies could not ignore the power of glamour. Hobnail boots acquired high heels. Queen's Freddy Mercury had his stage wear designed by Zandra Rhodes. Slade decked themselves in satin, adjusting their image to the mood of the moment rather than actually initiating a style.

Female glam rockers like Suzi Quatro were just as theatrical, although there was no hint of drag. Nona Hendryx of Labelle was one of the most glamorous. Her image was created by two American designers, Larry LeGaspi and Norma Kamali. LeGaspi employed shock tactics, and was inspired by space suits. The Martian look was emphasized by details of padding and quilting, combined with slinky fabrics and a body-stocking fit. LeGaspi's use of plumage hinted at the fantasy worlds of the Ziegfeld Follies and Busby Berkeley. Costume jewelry, designed by Richard Erker, completed the outfit.

▲Suzi Quatro abandoned her usual tight leathers for this metallic silver-look outfit. Quatro was one of the very first women to break the mold and play hard, driving rock and roll.

◄ Nona Hendryx of Labelle, dressed in silvery white, inspired by astronauts' clothing. The body stocking, quilting, and padding were elements of the fashion collections of Norma Kamali and Larry LeGaspi, the two designers behind Labelle's glamorous stage presence.

▲Freddie Mercury's fabulous stage outfits ranged from Zandra Rhodes commissions like this one to an antique Japanese kimono, a white satin jumpsuit, a leather basque, and spangled tights. Eyeliner and black nail polish on his right hand completed a truly glamorous image.

▶Debbie Harry's blend of streetwise style and cool sexuality found expression in a huge range of stage outfits from leather to high fashion.

Two other big-time female stage performers were American Chrissie Hynde of the British group The Pretenders and American Pat Benatar. Unlike Labelle, they modeled their costumes on those of male rock stars. Hynde put together unexpected combinations of hard and soft gear—ruffles with leather or lace gloves with a cut-down worn denim jacket. Her models were the foppish sixties group The Kinks and Robert Plant. Pat Benatar, on the other hand, combined disco-style spandex outfits and stiletto heels with macho metaphors drawn from heavy metal performances.

Dressed to Clash

Like Hell!

Possibly the most lasting image of the seventies has been punk. In 1976–77, punk got so much media attention that it has overshadowed the original American rock stage acts from which many elements of its style came. In early 1975, John Lydon (aka Johnny Rotten) adopted the short, spiky haircut that typifies punk—he had seen it in a photo of New York art band singer Richard Hell, who had invented the style in 1974. The New York Dolls and the Ramones, wearing jeans deliberately torn just below the knee, were very influential, as were Television, who wore their hair short in direct contrast to the hippies.

Many groups went even further than wild hairstyles with stage performances that often caused controversy. Alice Cooper, for instance, worked simulated killings into his performances during 1972.

▼John Lydon (aka Johnny Rotten of the Sex Pistols) in a Ben Sherman shirt, stenciled with lettering like an escaped convict's. The chains and studs applied to the deliberately ripped and torn, safety-pinned jacket, Maltese cross, and swastika were key elements in the punk look.

▲New York rock singer Richard Hell, whose short spiky hair—a prototype for the punk look—was adopted by John Lydon.

▶The New York Dolls playing around with gender and trying a few shock tactics, wearing makeup, women's blouses, and high-heeled, soft leather thigh boots.

But possibly the most individual act was that of The Tubes, from America's West Coast. In their stage show, the leader, Fee Waybill, wore metal-studded leather and an executioner's mask-helmet. His female assistant, Re Styles, was flung about the stage, wearing a black leather headpiece, corset, and strappy high-heeled shoes.

By 1977, the Mohican hairstyle—or Mohawk, taken from the Mohawk Indians—had become an identifying feature of punk youth. It was worn by Travis Bickle, played by Robert De Niro in Martin Scorsese's 1976 film *Taxi Driver*. The Mohawk looked downbeat, but in 1945, it had been a symbol of good luck worn by U.S. paratroopers. This overturning of contexts, giving new meaning to old ideas, was a vital aspect of fashion's shock tactics.

▼Punks hanging around London's Trafalgar Square in the mid-seventies. Despite punk's anti-fashion stance, what these young men are wearing represents an easily recognizable tribal uniform: carefully torn jeans, logo T-shirts, dyed Mohican hairstyles, and heavy leather boots.

Seditionaries

Punk may have begun in New York, but it was cleverly capitalized on in London by Malcolm McLaren and his partner, Vivienne Westwood. They sold "bondage trousers," with the legs strapped together behind the knees, at their World's End shop. Their clothes reflected the political argument that punk was somehow countercultural and rooted in the working classes.

Although often described as knowingly anarchic, the punk style was more often a meaningless assemblage of dog collars, safety pins, zippers, chains, school blazers, leather skirts, and ripped and torn shirts. The look was widely spread through album covers, posters, live performance of songs like The Sex Pistols' "Anarchy in the UK," and fanzines like *Sniffin' Glue*.

Priestesses of Punk

Punk is arguably one youth culture that involved women in a major way. There were a number of influential figures from the American rock scene—rock poet Patti Smith, for example, who wore layer upon layer of cardigans, men's shirts, ties, and big jackets, all of different lengths. Another look of hers included a loose-fitting, frumpish dress worn with heavy, unlaced work boots. She modeled her look on the clothes and attitude of male rock heroes, especially Keith Richards of The Rolling Stones, Bob Dylan, Jim Morrison, and Jimi Hendrix and on the French poet Rimbaud.

Another American, Debbie Harry, lead singer of Blondie, created a sensation early in her career through shock gimmicks in her stage act. She appeared in a New York nightclub wearing a white wedding dress and then ripped it off while belting out "Rip Her to Shreds."

◀ Top punk band The Clash, neatened up to look New Wave.

▲ Poly Styrene, of X-Ray Spex, subverting the conservatism of pastel-colored suits. The Lurex texture adds a hint of bad taste, while the headscarf is a defiant anti-glamour gesture. She flaunts the ultimate designer label: a charity store ticket pinned to one lapel.

Acts Lene Lovich and The Slits put outfits together from thrift shops, almost as if they were little girls playing dress-up, mixing tutus and Wellington boots and applying their makeup badly.

More sixties cast-offs, like skinny-rib sweaters and shift dresses and aggressively hard, shiny synthetic fabrics, were adopted by Fay Fife of the Rezillos, Pauline of Penetration, and Poly Styrene of X-Ray Spex. Ski pants or fishnet stockings completed some outfits. These band members asserted their sexual freedom and poked fun at the radical feminists' denouncement of fashion, while the B-52s played on a fifties cocktail-drinking society with their enormous wigs and secondhand glamour dresses.

Secondhand clothes, hair cut into weird shapes, and daring makeup were part of Siouxsie and the Banshees' image. Siouxsie Sioux's hacked haircut became a key element of the "Goth" look, which is now considered typically punk. In fact, it was more part of a New Wave stage act—pure attention seeking, with hints more of glamour than of shock. By the late seventies, New-Wave styles in fashion and music—a neater, brighter, and more commercial form of punk—entered the mainstream, taking over the hardcore black leather and plastic anarchic look. Thus, punk came to be seen as having more to do with fashion than with the subculture that it is sometimes made out to represent.

▼Siouxsie Sioux, dressed to kill. Her "gothic" makeup and hair were developed as a dramatic stage style, representing New Wave glamour rather than the radical, anarchic punk with which they are often mistakenly associated.

▲Punk girls showed that the boys didn't have things all their own way on the streets. The biker jacket was as much a unisex essential as the hairstyle, but was customized wherever possible with studs and pins.

Trash Culture

Cut Out the Garbage

Designers of new jewelry began turning away from precious metals and semiprecious stones and instead experimented with cheap materials, like nylon filament and acrylics. They were focusing on the design concept, new forms and meanings, and a celebration of bright color.

There were several reasons for this "trash culture." The latest technological breakthroughs in polymer science made available new kinds of plastic, which were much easier to manipulate and more wearable than they had been in the sixties. Built into them were new textures, weights, and color effects. A certain shock value could also be achieved by using cheap and cheerful substances conventionally associated with bad taste and with low or popular culture. And then there was the economic argument. With the seventies recession, designers had little money to invest in expensive materials, and although the buying public was hungry for novelty, people had limited funds. Fashion, too, played a big part—synthetic jewelry was the obvious accessory to artificial, Day-Glo hair colors.

By 1977, the spirit of nihilism, a rejection of current beliefs, and the influence of kitsch as self-conscious bad taste had filtered through the art colleges and into the fashion industry. Safety pins were used as jewelry. Brown parcel paper was cut out, varnished and manipulated into hair ornaments, brooches, and sophisticated pocketbooks. Toolboxes were used as handbags. Regular readers of *Cosmopolitan* sent in for the *Cosmo* clutch bag special offer—a cheap handbag of garish plastic, looking like a folded copy of the magazine itself.

Pinball Wizardry

The technicolor world of *The Wizard of Oz* came alive in the zany stage outfits of Elton John. His all-in-one suits of satin or brightly knitted material were decorated with cut-out stars and pom-

▲This green-and-red suede shoe with wraparound-tie ankle strap was designed by Manolo Blahnik in 1971 and used by Ossie Clark to complement a dress in his collection that year.

▼These Parisian men's jackets are printed with Pop Art images, including the iconic Andy Warhol-style soup cans.

◀ Many seventies clothes were far from flattering: here a knitted bodysuit with grimacing face and quilted and appliqué hot pants suit.

▲ Elton John had a wardrobe of glitter bodysuits and colored eyeglasses to go with them. This jacket, with spangled epaulets, was modeled on a circus ringmaster's tailcoat.

poms and worn with platform boots in a jigsaw of colors and shapes, sufficiently outrageous for walking down the "Yellow Brick Road." Eyeballs rolling within the frames of his glasses, some of which were illuminated by miniature flashing lightbulbs, he was a singing, dancing, jumping pinball machine come to life!

Plastic jeans, padded satin jackets with crass images in embroidery or appliqué, and lime green Lurex twelve-inch platform shoes: these were all part of the fun of hideous seventies "style." Many reacted with such revulsion that much of the "trash culture" was chucked into the garbage can rather than kept for museums of art and design.

But in addition to the garish, affordable end of this style, there were toned-down versions, especially in footwear. Classics included Chelsea Cobbler platform sandals decorated with bright-colored leather roses and Yves Saint Laurent rope-sole wedge espadrilles in primary colors, laced up the calf over tights of brightly clashing colors. The shoe designs of Manolo Blahnik and Maud Frizon showed how witty and innovative the unexpected mixture of materials could be—highly original, yet very much the spirit of the seventies.

The Fiorucci Phenomenon

▲ Fiorucci used striking images for its advertising campaigns in the 1970s. Here skintight pants are worn by topless models.

Elio Fiorucci was an Italian wizard who, by drawing on street culture, transformed the images of Pop Art and American graffiti into a highly successful retail business. Fiorucci corduroy jeans presented a bright spectrum of color that made the earlier seventies brushed denim and Levi's 501s look very drab.

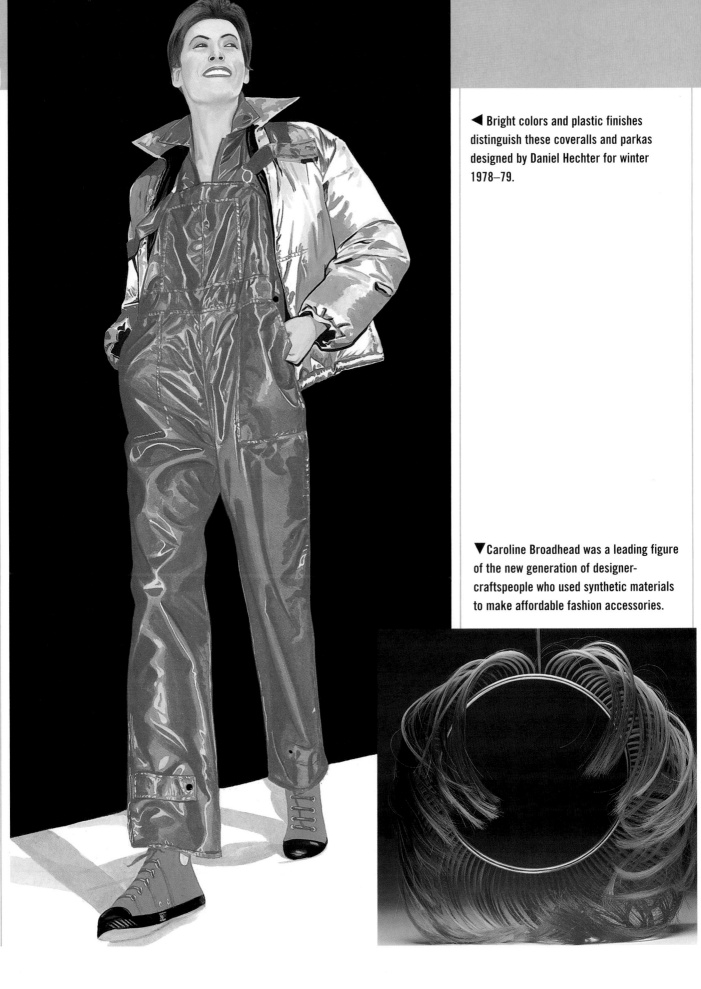

◀ Bright colors and plastic finishes distinguish these coveralls and parkas designed by Daniel Hechter for winter 1978–79.

▼Caroline Broadhead was a leading figure of the new generation of designer-craftspeople who used synthetic materials to make affordable fashion accessories.

Pockets were brashly zipped up with gold metal and decorated with printed plastic tags. Pink T-shirts printed with red, blue, and green and bright yellow stars or orange T-shirts printed with scarlet roses were fixed at the neck with woven Lurex Fiorucci labels.

This transfer-printed and airbrushed style was also applied to highly individualistic painted clothing and accessories like belts and ties. T-shirt graphics also carried messages in the language of popular culture or nonsensical splashes of sound-words picked out of comic-strip balloons, as in a late 1960s Roy Lichtenstein canvas or Richard Hamilton collage.

▲T-shirts featuring cartoons or defaced images, like this Sex Pistols "God Save the Queen" T-shirt, were very popular, and not just with punks.

▶This girl took her name, "Sue Catwoman," from her hairstyle. Her jacket has a deliberately synthetic appearance and is decorated with everyday trash objects.

Disco Kings and Queens

Body Stockings

The summer of 1970 was coined by the newspapers "the nudest ever." But the tiny bikinis and swimsuits of that year were nothing compared with the exaggeratedly high legs of 1976 or minimal swimsuits like the "String," the "Savage," and the "Thong," promoted by Los Angeles-based Rudi Gernreich, who was designing Lycra body wear for the French firm Lily.

The impression that the body had been spray-painted was created by the new range of leotards, worn for working out in the gym, for playing ball on the beach, or for disco dancing. One of the most innovative and successful manufacturers of leotards was Danskin, which marketed a collection of coordinating body wear, leotards with contrasting tights and wraparound skirts.

For disco dance wear young women wore leotards with all kinds of decoration: short frilled skirts, cap sleeves, spots, stripes, and rhinestones. These were also worn for exercise and for ice skating. They were sometimes worn with leg warmers, a feature that began as warm-up wear for the gym or in the dance studio and ended up as a fashion statement.

Hot pants—extra-skimpy shorts— were big news in the early seventies. Fashion writer for the *New Yorker* Kennedy Fraser noted: "Satin shorts are vulgar. Knitted shorts are nice, and crocheted shorts are delightful, but both are hard to wear." Hot pants of leather, suede, and velvet were generally considered okay and had the advantage of softening once worn in.

The new generation of designers who created "fun" clothing for teenagers included Americans Bill Blass and Geoffrey Beene. Youthful optimism was expressed in color, for this was one way to stand out from the established designers and the older generation. Yellow shorts next to purple tights were worn with orange platforms. Whether the hemline was maxi or mini, women

▼The obsession with exercise began in the seventies but would last throughout the next two decades, bringing fashion and sport closer than ever. Leotards, crop tops, hot pants, striped socks, and headbands were all soon hitting the streets.

▲Hot pants were not welcomed everywhere, as this young woman discovered when she tried to enter the exclusive—and very traditional—Royal Enclosure at Ascot races in her ultra-short outfit. She was politely turned away.

▲Jane Fonda's lean routine brought fun fitness into the living room. Everyone could join in her fast-moving workout program, either on television or through one of the many videos on sale.

of any age could indulge in a pair of colorful striped tights or over-the-knee socks—preferably clashing with the feet, which might be in scarlet work boots, emerald green square-toed sandals, or fuschia ankle boots.

Jogging Along

As jogging became a popular pastime, tracksuits arrived in a wide spectrum of colors. Coordinated headbands, frequently striped, were everywhere. Sportswear began to influence daytime clothing and party wear. In fact, the whole of fashion reflected the more informal lifestyle. This sense of ease was brilliantly expressed, under the Williwear label, by American designer Willi Smith.

As more and more sports stars turned professional, the business of sportswear design faced increased commercial pressure. Status was endorsed not by a label with the designer's name but by the sports star who promoted it. A whole new heraldry of sneaker logos was established—the Nike wave, the Converse star, the Adidas triple stripe, and the Puma flying wedge.

▲Sportswear was beginning to enter the fashion world. In this photo by Norman Parkinson, the model is wearing a leotard with matching candlewick cotton jacket and contrasting belt that draws attention to her slim waist.

◄ John Travolta, disco-dancing star of the film *Saturday Night Fever* and 1978's *Grease*. Not many bought the white suit, but hair gel came back in fashion in a big way when the first movie came out in 1977.

Roller Coasting

Around 1978, in hot pursuit of the skateboarding craze, roller skating and roller disco flashed onto the scene. Lycra and other stretchy, shiny fabrics were especially appropriate for these sports. Fashion designers were quick to latch onto this, producing a range of clothes to complement the skates. A typical example matched a pale pink satin vest (resembling a loose camisole), with boxer shorts and fuschia pink leather skating boots, worn with the obligatory headband.

Saturday Night Fever

The 1977 film *Saturday Night Fever* brought John Travolta into the limelight and put disco on the map. Travolta played dance-loving Brooklyn hardware store assistant Tony Manero in a story based on "Another Saturday Night," an article written by rock and pop chronicler Nik Cohn for *New York Magazine*. In his story, 2001 Odyssey is "the only disco in all Bay Ridge [Brooklyn] that truly counted." To qualify to dance there, "an aspirant need only be Italian, between the ages of eighteen and twenty-one, with a minimum stock of six floral shirts, four pairs of tight trousers, two pairs of Gucci-style loafers, two pairs of platforms, either a pendant or a ring, and one item in gold."

The formula was magic. It spawned a spate of feverish discomania, spin-off T-shirts and posters, and Travolta's next film, *Grease*.

▼ The roller-skating and skateboarding crazes sparked new fashion trends. Clothing that started off in the gym, then moved into the disco, was now brought right onto the streets of San Francisco.

The Rebirth of Style

Designer Labels

Early in the decade, Pierre Cardin, in whom so much faith had rested during the 1960s, was already being criticized for over-selling the franchise of his name. Other designers lost prestige by attaching their names to anything from suitcases to sheets.

Halston was one of America's first celebrity designers. Having outfitted Jackie Kennedy with her famous pill-box hats and clothed celebrities like Lauren Bacall, Liza Minnelli, and Bianca Jagger, in 1973, he signed a deal with Norton Simon, Inc., which purchased the right to use Halston's name on any product. This led to the launch of Max Factor's Halston scent.

The story was very different for newcomers to the designer label game. In 1978, Hirsch, the Manhattan entrepreneur behind Hong Kong jeans manufacturer Murjani, persuaded American socialite Gloria Vanderbilt to be photographed wearing jeans that bore her signature on a back pocket. The effect was instantaneous: in the first year, Murjani's sales multiplied six-fold. Women had grown tired of unisex, which made no allowances for curvy hips and concave waistlines. Vanderbilt persuaded women of the virtues of those designs dubbed with her name: "You don't have to lie on the floor to zip up my slacks, yet they are so constructed so they don't gape at the back."

In order to justify costing double or triple the price of regular jeans, designer jeans stood out from the rest of the crowd by the subtlest and least practical of details. Back pockets were omitted and quadruple seams introduced. But the greatest distinction was the designer's name fixed to a visible label. Calvin Klein and Pierre Cardin joined the designer jeans rat race, and Italian manufacturers were quick to produce cheaper versions, aimed at a younger market.

Back to the Classics

Following the 1973 oil crisis, men and women alike were economizing and investing in good-quality classics. Some of the famous ready-to-wear figures like Jean Muir, Sonia Rykiel, Diane Von Furstenberg, and Karl Lagerfeld of the Chloé boutique, succeeded in producing shapes inspired by classical drapery, which were simple and timeless, yet extremely difficult to imitate. Naturally, the distinction lay in the quality and

▲Plaid has always been a favorite in the fashion world. This outfit combines work by three of the major seventies talents. British designer Bill Gibb goes overboard with a plaid-and-check wool skirt worn with a printed cotton shirt. The ethnic-modern knitted waistcoat is by knitwear designer Kaffe Fassett, and the boots are by Chelsea Cobbler.

▼A selection of coats by Bonnie Cashin, one of America's most innovative designers. Some of her most famous lines were a wrapover patchwork coat, and several were based on the poncho, as seen here.

►Calvin Klein's tomato red linen jacket, white silk crepe blouse, and soft leather pants with elasticized waist and seams at the knee, featured in *Vogue* in 1979.

▼Issey Miyake's woolen cowboy look for winter 1978–79 is a good example of seventies experimentation in textured knitting.

fiber of the cloth, which justified the expense of even the simplest cut of top designer-made clothes.

By the mid-seventies, relative newcomers to the ready-to-wear scene—from America, Italy, and Japan, and, to a lesser extent, Britain, Germany, and Scandinavia—challenged the status quo and Paris couture with a more relaxed attitude to cut and construction. Newcomers to Paris included Issey Miyake, Yohji Yamamoto, Kansai Yamamoto, Rei Kawakubo of Comme des Garçons, Joseph Ettegui, and Kenzo of Jungle Jap.

Unstructured Elegance

In 1974, the focus of contemporary design moved away from the formal view of clothes—neat, stiffly structured suits and smart dresses with restaurant-length hemlines—toward a much softer "unconstructed" look. The concept involved the simplest cuts, which, deceptively, looked as if no skillful cutting was required. The unstructured look came increasingly to depend on the built-in drape and handle of jersey cloths, which could be made up quickly and economically but emulated the sophistication, body cling, and swirl of the pre-World War II bias cut. These garments showed off the body and were easy to wear and live in, but they also had style.

The mid-seventies pioneer of the unstructured jacket was Giorgio Armani of Milan, who set up his own business as design consultant in 1975 and soon began manufacturing his own ready-to-wear label. Armani's shoulders had a hard-edged, authoritative, executive width—no wonder he has often been described as the champion of women's power dressing, which began in the seventies. That apparently loose elegance, although in a more witty, relaxed form, was created by Ralph Lauren and modeled by Diane Keaton in the film *Annie Hall* (1977).

In fact, in the following decade, the wearing of a suit was to become the name of the game for all men and women determined to get ahead.

▲Diane Keaton makes Ralph Lauren menswear sexy for women in Woody Allen's comedy *Annie Hall*. Lauren's mix-and-match casuals were easy to wear and radiated Old World confidence.

▲Nino Cerutti, founder of the family tailoring firm, wearing one of his own suits in 1972.

◀ Giorgio Armani fits a jacket on one of his male models at the 1979 Milan fashion show.

▲Two outfits by Japanese designer Kenzo Takada. Both feature dresses in multicolored printed cotton, worn with *(left)* a broad sash and scarf and *(right)* red cotton pants. Both models wear ethnic wooden jewelry.

▲Classic elegance from one of the masters of simplicity, Jean Muir. This flowing red dress is given a touch of modernity, however, by the unusual footwear.

◄ An elegant but practical line of the late 1970s by Karl Lagerfeld, who designed under the Chloé label. An interest in pliable knitted textures, garments constructed from few pieces, and off-beat colors were typical of the decade.

Chronology

News

1970 US invades Cambodia.
National Guard kill four anti-war protesters at Kent State University, Ohio.
US celebrates first Earth Day.
Five planes hijacked by Palestinian Black September guerrillas.

1971 First Strategic Arms Limitation Treaty (SALT) agreement at Moscow summit.
War between India and Pakistan.
Nation of Bangladesh is created.
Police storm Attica prison in NY State: 42 dead.

1972 US President Richard Nixon visits Beijing, China.
Berlin Wall opened to allow family visits.
Leaders of Baader-Meinhof gang arrested in Germany.
Murder of Israeli athletes by Black September terrorists at Munich Olympics.

1973 Vietnam cease-fire; US troops withdrawn; military draft ends.
Military coup in Chile.
Yom Kippur Arab-Israeli war; Arab states raise oil prices and embargo oil to US.
Israel and Egypt declare cease-fire; Middle East peace talks open in Geneva.

1974 India explodes its first atom bomb.
Civil war breaks out in Cyprus.
British mainland bombings by IRA.
US President Richard Nixon resigns.

1975 Communists take over Cambodia and South Vietnam; last Americans leave as Saigon falls.
Mozambique and Angola become independent.
Emperor Haile Selassie dies.
Civil war in Lebanon and Angola.

1976 United States observes Bicentennial.
Airline passengers hijacked at Entebbe, Uganda, by PFLP guerrillas.
Riots in Soweto, South Africa.
Mao Ze-dong dies.

1977 Charter 77, human rights manifesto, published in Czechoslovakia.
Steve Biko dies in police custody in South Africa.
Hijacking of plane by Baader-Meinhof terrorists in Somalia.
Egyptian president Anwar Sadat visits Israel.

1978 Amoco Cadiz disaster results in massive oil slick in English Channel.
Menachem Begin and Anwar Sadat agree to Camp David Accords for Middle East peace.
Diplomatic relations opened between US and People's Republic of China.

1979 Shah of Iran abdicates: Iran becomes Islamic Republic: US embassy seized and staff taken hostage.
Vietnamese depose Pol Pot regime in Kampuchea (Cambodia).
Margaret Thatcher becomes British prime minister.
Russians invade Afghanistan.

Events

Isle of Wight festival "of music and love" opens in Britain: Jimi Hendrix's last public appearance.
Movie *M*A*S*H*, starring Donald Sutherland and Elliot Gould, premieres.
First cheap pocket calculators retailed in US.

A Clockwork Orange, Love Story, and, onstage, *Jesus Christ Superstar.*
George Harrison promotes Bangladesh Benefit Concert in Central Park.
Britain's currency converts to decimal system.
Jim Morrison, lead singer of The Doors, dies.

David Bowie's *Ziggy Stardust* album.
Rocky Horror Show hits the stage.
US bans use of pesticide DDT.

American baseball star Roberto Clemente dies.
Senate opens Watergate hearings.

Alexander Solzhenitsyn goes into exile in the West.
Spoof western *Blazing Saddles* opens.
North Sea oil begins to flow.

Blockbuster movie *Jaws* released.
International Women's Year proclaimed; Sex Discrimination Act introduced in Britain.
Bruce Springsteen's first hit, "Born to Run," released.

Race Relations Act introduced in Britain.
Extremist right-wing National Front confrontation at Notting Hill Carnival, London.
Gases from spray cans reported to damage the ozone layer.

London-New York passenger service on Concorde jet begins.
Sex Pistols' "God Save the Queen" banned by BBC.
Elvis Presley dies.

World's first test tube baby born.
"Winter of Discontent" grips Britain as unions strike for substantial wage settlements.
Marathon running turns into big public events.

Sex Pistol Sid Vicious dies from drug overdose while awaiting trial for alleged murder.
Woody Allen's movie *Manhattan.*

Fashions

Launch of *W*, a new paper for "the beautiful people."
Corduroy jeans and skin-tight, ribbed sweaters: leather beaded chokers and bracelets: striped sweatbands for sporty types, bandannas and Indian block-prints for hippies.

Hot pants galore, in satin and velvet, sometimes worn with maxi-length coats: cartridge belts for would-be cowboys and heavy-metal musicians.

Widely flared bell bottom pants: 1920s and 1940s revival clothes at Biba in London: handpainted leather bags, silk shirts, appliqué: pants tucked into knee-length boots: colorful cropped sleeveless pullovers.

Glam shiny suits and make-up for men on stage: embroidered kaftans, Indian shirts and gauze smocks: simply cut dresses in new synthetic jersey: boom in T-shirts printed with political and advertising slogans.
American Lauren Hutton becomes highest paid model in history.

"Granny" clothes and collarless "grandfather" shirts: suede "creeper" shoes with thick soles as part of the rock 'n' roll revival.
Designer knitwear boosts interest in hand-knitting and picture sweaters.

Cheap and radical chic: second-hand baseball jackets: army fatigues in khaki camouflage: Fiorucci fun clothing: clingy dresses flaring just below the knee: fake furs gain popularity in face of anti-fur lobbying.
Giorgio Armani sets up on his own as design consultant.

Exercise clothing and Lycra leotards.
Punk Festival at London's 100 Club.
Expansion of clothing and textile manufacture in developing countries.

Punk anarchy: safety pins, ripped and torn second-hand clothes, plastic, leather.
Diane Keaton wears Ralph Lauren trouser suits for Woody Allen movie *Annie Hall.*

Women's executive fashion: tailored coats, "unconstructed" jackets and padded shoulders.
Punk style glamorized and tamed in new wave fashion.

More than 30 brands of designer label jeans are on the market.
"New Romantic" fantasy dressing takes hold.
Sony Walkman introduced.

Glossary

Armani, Giorgio (b. 1935) Italian designer. Worked for menswear manufacturer Nino Cerruti in 1960s. Set up own consultancy in 1975, working for several companies, including Emanuel Ungaro, before establishing Armani fashion label.

Ashley, Laura (1925-85) British designer and manufacturer. Company, based in Wales, produced Victorian and Edwardian-style dresses of printed cottons with a country look. During 1970s, shops opened worldwide.

Beene, Geoffrey (1927-2004) American designer. Trained in United States and Paris. Began ready-to-wear in 1963; less expensive line called "Beene Bag."

Biba Mail order business set up in 1963 by Barbara Hulanicki, which soon developed into London's Biba boutique. In 1973 took over Art Deco department store in London. Known for nostalgic, moody clothes.

Blass, Bill (1922-2002) American designer of sportswear whose practical approach to fashion permeates his softer, more luxurious evening garments.

Cardin, Pierre (b. 1922) French designer. Worked for Paquin, Schiaparelli and Dior before launching his first womenswear collection in 1957, followed in 1963 by ready-to-wear. During the 1970s Cardin expanded the franchising of his name and business.

Djellabah Moroccan hooded cloak with long, wide sleeves, worn open at the neck and reaching to the knee.

Fiorucci, Elio (b. 1935) Italian designer and retailer. Established his own house in the 1960s but best known in the 1970s for bright, fun clothing, including slimfit jeans, sold internationally at Fiorucci boutiques.

Gibb, Bill (b. 1943) British designer. Set up his own company in 1972, with retail business from 1975. Best known for evening dresses in floaty and exotic fabrics, sometimes with appliqué or embroidery.

Halston (1932-1990) American milliner turned clothing designer. Dressed Jackie Kennedy from the 1960s and created simple ready-to-wear knitwear and elegant sportsclothes of jersey fabrics through 1970s. One of the first big American names to franchise his label.

Hechter, Daniel (b. 1938) French designer. Known for rain-, duffle- and greatcoats with a difference (e.g., made of jersey), sporty blazers and divided skirts.

Johnson, Betsey (b. 1942) American designer. Created extravagant disco wear in the 1970s and opened her own sportswear business in 1978.

Kamali, Norma (b. 1945) American designer. Known for cheerleader skirts, glamorous bodysuits and easy, extra-light coats and suits, using industrial and active sports fabrics like parachute nylon and sweatshirting.

Kawakubo, Rei (b. 1942) Japanese designer behind Comme des Garçons, formed in 1969. Favors somber colors and deliberately disheveled, draped clothes in reaction against traditional ideas of femininity.

Kenzo (b. 1940) Japanese designer, born Kenzo Takada. Freelance designer for Louis Feraud in 1960s Paris. In 1970 he opened his own Jungle Jap shop. Known for dynamic layers and mixtures of patterns and bright colors, inspired by traditional and folk dress.

Klein, Calvin (b. 1942) American designer. After working for New York manufacturers of coats and suits, set up his own sportswear business in 1968. During the 1970s, clothes became increasingly sophisticated; sleek lines and soft and crisp fabrics of silk, linen and fine suede.

Lagerfeld, Karl (b. 1938) German born, but career based in Paris. Designed freelance for Krizia, Charles Jourdan and Fendi. Throughout the 1970s, particularly associated with Chloé ready-to-wear collections.

Lauren, Ralph (b. 1939) American designer. Worked for Brooks Brothers, then Beau Brummel neckwear. In 1968, launched Polo line of menswear, and from 1971 produced womenswear collections, including designer jeans and in 1978 the "Prairie" look.

Missoni Italian family-run company founded 1953. Raised profile of knitwear in 1970s through boldly patterned long cardigans and sophisticated sweaters for men and women.

Miyake, Issey (b. 1935) Japanese designer. Studied fashion in Paris; worked for Guy Laroche, Hubert de Givenchy and Geoffrey Beene. Held first fashion show in New York, 1971; the next in Paris, 1973.

Mori, Hanae (b. 1926) Japanese designer. Opened New York salon in early 1970s, and in 1977 showed first couture collection in Paris. Design ideas influenced by traditional Japanese kimono and obi (sash).

Muir, Jean (1928-1995) British designer. Trademark classic clothes made of heavyweight rayon jerseys and punched and stitched suede.

Porter, Thea (1927-2000) British designer. In the 1960s sold antique Near Eastern textiles from London shop and began designing "ethnic" clothes from exotic fabrics for evening wear. Opened a New York store in1968, and one in Paris in early 1970s.

Price, Antony (b. 1945) British designer. Designs for Bryan Ferry and Roxy Music brought success by mid-1970s, and in 1979 launched his own label.

Rykiel, Sonia (b. 1930) French designer. Known in the 1970s mostly for knitwear in subtle colors of beige, gray and slate blue.

Saint Laurent, Yves (b. 1936) French designer. Former chief designer at Dior, established his own house in 1962. In 1970s designed impeccably cut suits: some inspired by exotic Eastern and Russian sources, some more sober for the new executive woman.

Smith, Willi (1948-1991) American designer of ethnic-influenced sportswear inspired by trips to India. Set up Willi Wear casual sportswear in 1976.

Von Furstenberg, Diane (b. 1946) Belgian born. Apprenticed in 1968 to Italian textile manufacturer Angelo Ferretti and opened her own business in New York in 1972. Known for plain, simply cut or wrap printed silk jersey dresses.

Yuki (b. 1937) Japanese designer, born Gnyuki Torimaru. Worked for Louis Feraud, Norman Hartnell and Pierre Cardin before designing collections under his own name from 1973. In 1970s designed one-size jersey dresses of tubes and rectangles, made fluid through draping and the movement of the body.

Further Reading

A great deal has been written and published about the 1970s, and this reading list is only a very small selection. Magazines and movies of the period are another excellent source of information.

Adult General Reference Sources

Calasibetta, Charlotte. *Essential Terms of Fashion: A Collection of Definitions* (Fairchild, 1985)

Calasibetta, Charlotte. *Fairchild's Dictionary of Fashion*, (Fairchild, 2nd ed,1988)

Cumming, Valerie. *Understanding Fashion History* (Chrysalis, 2004)

Ewing, Elizabeth. *History of Twentieth Century Fashion*, revised by Alice Mackrell (Batsford, 4th ed, 2001)

Gold, Annalee. *90 Years of Fashion* (Fairchild, 1990)

Laver, James. *Costume and Fashion* (Thames & Hudson, 1995)

Martin, Richard. *American Ingenuity: Sportswear 1930s–1970s* (Yale, 1998)

O'Hara, Georgina. *The Encyclopedia of Fashion* (Harry N. Abrams, 1986)

Peacock, John. *Men's Fashion: The Complete Sourcebook* (Emerald, 1997)

Peacock, John. *Fashion Accessories: The Complete 20th Century Sourcebook* (Thames & Hudson, 2000)

Polhemus, Ted and Procter, L. *Fashion and Anti-Fashion* (Thames & Hudson, 1978)

Skinner, Tina. *Fashionable Clothing from Sears Catalogs* (Schiffer, 2004)

Steele, Valerie. *Fifty Years of Fashion: New Look to Now* (Yale, 2000)

Stegemeyer, Anne. *Who's Who in Fashion*, (Fairchild, 4th ed, 2003)

Trahey, Jane (ed.) Harper's Bazaar: *100 Years of the American Female* (Random House, 1967)

Watson, Linda. *Twentieth-century Fashion* (Firefly, 2004)

Adult General Reference Sources

Gilmour, Sarah. *Twentieth Century Fashion: the 70s* (Heinemann Library, 1999)

Ruby, Jennifer. *The 1960s & 1970s*, Costume in Context series (David & Charles, 1989)

Wilcox, R. Turner. *Five Centuries of American Costume* (Scribner's, 1963).

Young Adult Sources

Gilmour, Sarah. *Twentieth Century Fashion: the 70s* (Heinemann Library, 1999)

Ruby, Jennifer. *The 1960s & 1970s*, Costume in Context series (David & Charles, 1989)

Wilcox, R. Turner. *Five Centuries of American Costume* (Scribner's, 1963).

Acknowledgments

The Publishers would like to thank the following for permission to reproduce illustrations: Bath Museum 20t, 59tl; B.T. Batsford 10l, 12l, 26r, 30r, 34t, 36l, 42r, 44l, 49tl, 50l, 52, 54b, 57r, 59bl, 59r; BFI Stills 6; Camera Press 11l, 24, 32, 34b, 54t; Caroline Broadhead 50r; FIT 56b; Getty 9l, 17r, 19, 25r, 35; Getty/Time Life 58l; Popperfoto 10r, 15, 53r; Retro Library 26l; Rex Features 8l, 9r, 12r, 13, 14, 16, 17l, 18l, 20b, 21, 23, 25l, 28, 30l, 33, 36r, 37, 38, 39, 40, 41, 42l, 43r, 44r, 45t, 46, 47l, 48, 49bl, 49r, 51, 53l, 55, 56t, 57l, 58tr, ; Topfoto 7, 8r, 22, 27, 29, 31, 43l, 45b, 47r; Victoria & Albert Museum 11r, 18r

Key: b=bottom, t=top, l=left, r=right

Index

Figures in *italics* refer to illustrations.